SLP Past and Present

53 YEARS SINCE
THE END OF STEAM
1968 **53** 2021

Railways & Recollections
THE END OF BR steam 1968
John Stretton and Peter Townsend

Contents

Acknowledgements

Silver Link Books
Mortons Media Group Limited
Media Centre
Morton Way
Horncastle
LN9 6JR

Tel/Fax: 01507 529535
email: sohara@mortons.co.uk
Website: www.nostalgiacollection.com

Printed and bound in the Czech Republic

© John Stretton and Peter Townsend 2020

First published in 2021

ISBN 978 1 85794 525 6

British Library Cataloguing in Publication Data. A catalogue record for this book is available from the British Library.

Your authors have always derived great pleasure from our railways, their history, geography, motive power and enduring illustrations. We have compiled a number of books together, including *Railways & Recollections* volumes, but this one is special, for not only does it have views of the last months of BR steam – and a few 'wilderness' months thereafter – but we are also able to dedicate it to a very talented and supportive man, who was always willing to help.

As always we could not have made the book what it is without the assistance of others. In particular (and sometimes by extension) we thank Connie Ruffell, Will Adams, Chris Milner (Editor of *The Railway Magazine*), Phil Horton, Colin Marsden, Peter Simmonds, Peter Fitton, Gerald Adams, Roger Thwaites, the Armstrong Railway Photographic Trust and the many railwaymen who tolerated and accommodated the many hundreds who 'invaded' the North West in search of the last puffs of smoke!

Dedication

During the preparation of this volume, Peter Skelton, who had been helping us with sourcing some photographs, very sadly died suddenly. He was a widely acknowledged and respected photographer in his own right and he is greatly missed by his friends and colleagues, not least in the TYMCARS. Our love and sympathy go out to his wife Danuta and his family at this time, and this volume is dedicated to him.

Title page: **BOLTON** This image, captured by your co-author on 2 August 1968, encapsulates so much of the essence of the steam age railway that was about to be swept away, to be, it was thought, consigned to the pages of history. But the lone locospotter with his notebook, in which he would record his sightings, was not to know that this was far from the end of steam! Over 8 million people a year visit heritage railways, paying homage to the era that truly was 'the steam age' railway.

The silent line of locomotives is headed by ex-LMS Class 8F 2-8-0 No 48319. Although silent now, this locomotive had travelled far and wide having been based at Rose Grove (24B), Barrow Hill (18D), Wellingborough (15A), Saltley (21A), Toton (18A), Nottingham (16A), Fleetwood (10C), Springs Branch (8F), Patricroft, (9H), Heaton Mersey (9F) and Bolton (9K), from where it was sent for scrapping during October 1968 (See also Page 30). *MJS*

Introduction

I 968 was certainly a momentous year with world politics taking centre stage. In January the 'Prague Spring' in Czechoslovakia saw Alexander Dubcek elected as the secretary of the country's Communist Party replacing Antonin Novotny. Dubcek introduced a more liberal form of government, moving away from Stalinist policies. The change was not to last; Soviet armed forces invaded and occupied Czechoslovakia in August and Dubcek was deposed in April 1969.

North Korea meanwhile captured the USS *Pueblo* and its 83 crew, causing heightened tensions between the two countries, some 15 years after the end of the Korean War. Negotiations resulted in the release of the crew from the POW camp in which they had been held. The war in Vietnam raged on with the North Vietnamese launching what became known as the Tet Offensive, which proved costly for

the US and South Vietnamese, who were caught out by the surprise attacks spread across the country. Over 500 US soldiers were killed in a single week in early February and over 2,500 were injured! This was to prove a turning point, with US citizens seeing the horrors of war on their TV screens, prompting extensive campaigning and demonstrations calling for an end to the war.

On 5 April Dr Martin Luther King, a leading Civil Rights activist, was assassinated while standing on the balcony of his Memphis motel room the night after his now famous 'I've seen the Promised Land' sermon. US President Lyndon B. Johnson became increasingly isolated and declared later in the year that he would not stand in the Presidential election. Robert F. Kennedy won the California primary and was set to win the Democratic Presidential nomination, but was assassinated by Sirhan Sirhan, a Jordanian immigrant, as he left the Ambassador Hotel on 5 June.

Closer to home, here in the UK the hugely popular Ford Anglia was finally consigned to motoring history, replaced in January with the soon to prove as popular Ford Escort. The 'I'm Backing Britain' campaign was endorsed by Prime Minister Harold Wilson. The PM also announced the standing down of the UK Civil Defence Corps, established back in 1949 as a force to be called upon in a national emergency. Percy Thrower, the much-loved gardening expert, appeared for the first

time on the long-running *Gardener's World* on BBC 1; also screened for the first time later in the year was *Dad's Army*. Motor-racing favourite Jim Clark was killed while taking part in a Formula 2 race at Hockenheim on 7 April. On 20 April Enoch Powell made his controversial 'Rivers of Blood' speech on immigration and was dismissed from Edward Heath's shadow cabinet the following day. The Church of Scotland allowed the ordination of female ministers for the first time.

Frederick West became Britain's first heart transplant patient, living for just 46 days following the operation. The first Isle of Wight Festival took place in August, and the Post Office introduced the first and second class postal service the following month. Moving on to the main subject of this volume, we find that the only area still operating steam on the national network at the start of the year was the North West. Steam had been disappearing at an increasingly rapid rate, with the Western Region being first to be 'steam free' by the close of 1965 and the Southern Region by the end of 1967, leaving just parts of the Midland and Eastern Regions, where steam had also disappeared by the end of August 1968. Locomotives during this period were being despatched to scrapyards all over the country at a rapidly increasing rate, and examples can be seen in these introductory pages. As can be seen in this volume, the passion for steam month by month during the year became something of a

BARRY DOCKS The sun shines brightly on No 5322, but its future appears to be bleak as it stands in a line of other withdrawn locomotives in January 1968. New from Swindon Works on 20 August 1917, at a cost of £3,783, it was withdrawn from Pontypool Road shed in April 1964 and found its way to Woodham Brothers' yard the following year. Its eventful career began immediately after building, with a move from Swindon to France, for the War Department, where it stayed until May 1919. In 1928, along with 64 others of the class, it was amended for weight distribution and renumbered 8322. This lasted until June 1944, when it reverted to its original design as No 5322. Fitted with outside steam pipes in 1949, it received its last Heavy Intermediate overhaul, at Wolverhampton Stafford Road Works, in May 1961. It amassed 1,355,622-plus miles in its time and was the third loco to leave Barry, in 1969, to be preserved at GWS, Didcot. *MJS collection*

challenge, with enthusiasts chasing their beloved locomotives where'er they may roam. The last few steam sheds at Buxton, Bolton, Rose Grove and Lostock Hall became Meccas. The shed staff were for the most part found to be friendly and accommodating, even allowing groups to clean the locomotives running the last few steam turns!

Then end finally came on 11 August 1968 with the running of 1T57 - the 'Fifteen Guinea Special' – so named from the cost of a ticket. This

train ran from Liverpool to Carlisle via Manchester. The month of August in this volume is therefore understandably rather longer than the other months in the year!

In fact, this was not quite the end of steam on Britain's railways. British Rail still owned and operated three narrow-gauge locomotives on the

Vale of Rheidol line from Aberystwyth to Devil's Bridge (now privately owned and still running today). Parts of Northern Ireland Railways operated steam until 1971, and Alan Pegler's *Flying Scotsman*, purchased from BR in 1963, had an exemption clause in the contract of purchase that allowed it to run on the main-line network in spite of the steam ban

BARRY DOCKS is seen again on 17 March 1968. The influx of engines over the previous few years led to lines of stored locos, and opportunities for some different camera angles. Ex-GWR 2-6-2T No 4141 is seen head-on, trapped between spent coal and a long line stretching out behind it. New in 1946, its operational life was relatively short, being withdrawn in March 1963. However, preservation beckoned in 1973 and it has since worked on both the Severn Valley and Great Central railways.

Above: Through the looking glass!

Above right: LMS tanks Nos 47357 and 41312 stand with ex-SR No 35005 *Canadian Pacific* in deepest Wales! All survived into preservation, in 1970, 1974 and 1973 respectively.

Right: Two more to survive, Nos 73082 and 35022 *Holland-America Line*, both entered the yard in 1966 and left in 1979 and 1986. *All MJS*

introduced by BR on 12 August 1968. The ban was in reality only to last for three years, ex-GWR locomotive No 6000 *King George V* being the first to run once more on the BR network. The months following the end of steam saw a dramatic fall in photographic activity by railway enthusiasts. It was as if railway enthusiasm itself was in danger of disappearing! The scarcity now of, for example, images of two-tone-green diesels bears this out. Thus, the later months are somewhat shorter in this volume, having 'donated' space for the steam age period.   We trust you will enjoy the nostalgia herein, albeit tinged with sadness perhaps, and come back to another volume in the series very soon!

John Stretton   Ashchurch

Peter Townsend   Kettering

August 2020

BARRY DOCKS There have been many shots of the numerous locos at Barry Docks over the years at the height of the collection, but none portrays the layout of the display of the sheer number of types present as this semi-aerial view of the West Pond site in early 1968. Among others are Nos 92214 and 3850. The former was just six years old when withdrawn (from Severn Tunnel Junction) and entering the yard in 1965. It was a further 15 years before release and a journey to the Peak Rail Society at Buxton. No 3850, also withdrawn in 1965 (from Croes Newydd shed), was born in 1942. Its rescue came in 1984 by the West Somerset Railway. *MJS collection*

Above left: **BARRY DOCKS** Spotter Roger Thwaites momentarily has his attention attracted away from ex-GWR locos Nos 3862, 4156, 4110, 9682, 4144, 9681, 4612 and 3738 in the dull conditions at Barry Docks on 17 March 1968. All had arrived here in 1965.

Above **NEWPORT** J. Cashmore's scrapyard in Newport saw the end of numerous locos during the slaughter of ex-BR stock, and No 45188 is seen pending the final cut, newly arrived on 17 March 1968. New from Armstrong Whitworth in September 1935 as LMS No 5188, it was renumbered by BR in July 1949. Its final home, until July 1967, had been Speke Junction shed, near Liverpool.

Left: **BARRY DOCKS** Of newer construction than most in the yard on 17 March 1968, 'twins' Nos 78019 and 78018 have the attention of another enthusiast. Constructed at Darlington Works in early 1954, both were withdrawn in 1966 and entered the yard the following year. '19' left in March 1973 and '18' some five years later in October 1978, and both have steamed at a number of preservation sites since, occasionally reunited. *All MJS*

January

Right: **READING GENERAL** Paddington or Waterloo – the choice is yours on 6 January! On the left is a 2HAL unit destined to take the Southern route to London Waterloo, south of the River Thames, while on the right passengers could take the quicker Western Region route to London Paddington and finish up north of the river behind 'Western' Class 52 No D1002 *Western Explorer*. Modellers may care to note the motley collection of rolling stock behind the 'Western', with maroon and blue and grey liveries in evidence.
Ray Ruffell/Slip Coach PS Ltd Archive

Right: **ALTON** On 20 January to the left is the newly delivered HB/Class 74 No E6102 on test. This was one of 10 locomotives rebuilt as electro-diesels at Crewe Works during 1967-68 from earlier HA/Class 71s built at Doncaster Works and introduced as far back as 1958. In the centre road is DEMU No 1121; introduced in 1958, this unit lasted until October 1993 when it was withdrawn in Network SouthEast livery. Saved from the cutter's torch, DTC No 60820 from this unit can at the time of writing be found at the Lavender Line on loan from Hastings Diesels Limited. On the right is HAP unit No 6014 bound for Waterloo.
Ray Ruffell/Slip Coach PS Ltd ArchiveFar

Right top: **FARNHAM** The aforementioned No E6102 electro-diesel is seen at Snails Lynch siding undergoing brake trials attached to DTSO No 76331.

Right: **ALTON** No E6102 failed at Alton on 30 January and Class 33 No D6510 was sent to rescue both the loco and DTSO No 76331, returning them to Farnham. *Ray Ruffell/Slip Coach PS Ltd Archive*

February: Buxton area

Below: **BUXTON** There is just one week to go before Buxton's steam shed will close, yet there is still a considerable number of locomotives to be seen. This view, taken on 24 February from the coaling stage, provides an impression of the extent of the shed yard. The coaling chute used to fill the tenders and bunkers is clearly visible, but it will not be dispensing the life blood of the firebox for very much longer! *Ray Ruffell/Slip Coach PS Ltd Archive*

Above right: **BUXTON** Two Stanier LMS taper-boiler Class 8F 2-8-0s Nos 48471 and 48424 stand side by side over the pits outside Buxton shed on 24 February. No 48471 had been based at Buxton since November 1967, having arrived from Newton Heath. Following closure of Buxton, a brief allocation to Heaton Mersey shed beckoned, from where withdrawal took place in April 1968. Interestingly No 48424 is recorded as being withdrawn from service on the day this photograph was taken. During June 1968 the loco was scrapped at Cohens yard in Kettering. *Ray Ruffell/Slip Coach PS Ltd Archive*

Right: **BUXTON** Another view taken shortly after the image at the foot of the previous page shows No 48191 continuing the process of shunting the stock to make up a train ready for departure from Buxton yard. *Ray Ruffell/Slip Coach Ltd ArchiveBottom*

Below right: **BUXTON** Stanier 8F No 48775 takes a breather at Buxton on 24 February 1968. Built at Crewe Works in 1937, this loco was first destined for service with the War Department, carrying the number 70512. In 1957 it was purchased by British Railways and became a resident of the Scottish shed at Glasgow Polmadie (66A). Having been withdrawn and reinstated twice during 1962/63, this ardent survivor fetched up at Carlisle (Kingmoor) (12A), Newton Heath (26A), Agecroft (26B), and Patricroft. *Ray Ruffell/Slip Coach PS Ltd Archive*

Left: **BUXTON** Another Class 8F 2-8-0, Rose Grove-based No 48191, is seen shunting LMS 20T brake van No M730866 in Buxton yards on the same day. The loco is looking well cared for, possibly having been cleaned by enthusiasts in recent days. It was to last a while longer, being withdrawn from Rose Grove shed right at the end of steam on 3 August 1968. The brake van is of particular interest; having survived the cutter's torch, at the time of writing it can be seen on the Severn Valley Railway. *Ray Ruffell/Slip Coach PS Ltd Archive*

Above: **STOCKPORT** Ex-LMS Stanier 8F 2-8-0 No 48182 stands on shed at Stockport Edgeley (9B) on 24 February in front of the LNWR water tower. The loco was living on borrowed time, being withdrawn from service just three months later. *Ray Ruffell/Slip Coach PS Ltd ArchiveRight:*

STOCKPORT The past meets the future at Stockport Edgeley station on 24 February as ex-LMS Stanier 'Black 5' 4-6-0 No 44836 passes Bo-Bo No E3010. It is interesting to note that No 44836 was in service for less time than No E3010 by some four years.
Ray Ruffell/Slip Coach PS Ltd Archive

Left: **ROSE GROVE** On 23 March two ex-LMS Stanier 'Black 5s' are seen from inside the shed. On the left is No 48257, while outside next to the water columns is No 48491. By this stage the shed roads were far less busy than in the days when steam ruled on Britain's railways – the inspection pits seen here would have been seeing far more use! *Ray Ruffell/Slip Coach PS Ltd Archive Above:*

ROSE GROVE Ex-LMS 'Black 5' 4-6-0 No 44848 seen here on 23 March was a much-travelled example of the class, having spent time at several sheds including Saltley, Carlisle Kingmoor, Derby, Leicester (Midland), Leicester (Great Central), Annesley, Colwick and finally Rose Grove, from where it had been withdrawn the month prior to this photo being taken. The loco's final passing took place at Cohens yards near Kettering, Northamptonshire. *Ray Ruffell/Slip Coach PS Ltd Archive*

Below: **ROSE GROVE** A general view of the shed on 23 March shows various unidentified 8F locos in steam awaiting their next tour of duty. No 48448 can be identified standing next to the right-hand water column. *Ray Ruffell/Slip Coach PS Ltd Archive*

ROSE GROVE Ex-LMS Class 8F 2-8-0 (or should that be 0-8-0?) No 48375 stands forlornly at the end of a siding following an accident at Copy Pit, which may well explain why it is minus its front bogie. No 48375 was withdrawn in September/October 1967 and would be cut up at Rose Grove the following month. *Ray Ruffell/Slip Coach PS Ltd Archive Right:*

Above: **ROSE GROVE** From just outside the shed Ray Ruffell captured this fine study of a locomotive in its final year of life, grimy, weary and weathered. Yet 8F Class 2-8-0 No 48491 still somehow manages to stand majestic on a cold, wet and miserable 23 March 1968. To the left stands the previously seen 8F No 48448.
Ray Ruffell/Slip Coach PS Ltd Archive

Above right: **BOLTON** Moving to Bolton shed we find a dedicated railwayman busy cleaning 'Black 5' 4-6-0 No 45260. Your authors could find no references to a rail tour taking place in the days following 23 March, so it would seem that this is a fine example of the pride taken in the job even at this late stage of the steam age!
Ray Ruffell/Slip Coach PS Ltd Archive

Right: **BOLTON** A rare shot of Ray Ruffell in front of the camera rather than behind it! He is standing next to BR Standard Class 5 4-6-0 No 73040 and 'Black 5' 4-6-0 No 44929.
Ray Ruffell/Slip Coach PS Ltd Archive

ROSE GROVE An atmospheric shot of 8F Class No 48666 passing Rose Grove with a heavy coal train on 23 March. The condition of the majority of the surviving steam locomotives at this time can be clearly seen in this shot, with considerable leakage of steam evident and an all-round lack of TLC!
Ray Ruffell/Slip Coach PS Ltd Archive

Above: **BARRY DOCKS** Another slightly artistic shot, this time utilising sundry abandoned equipment on 17 March 1968. Though from the same class and superficially the same, No 4110 (centre) was new from Swindon Works in 1936, whereas No 4156 behind it was from a totally different batch, not seeing the light of day until August 1947, only just still in the GWR era. While both were withdrawn from Severn Tunnel Junction shed in June 1965, No 4110 went on to see preservation (initially to the ex-BR shed at Southall), but No 4156 became one of the relatively few actually cut up by Woodham Brothers, by July 1980.

Above right: **BARRY DOCKS** Another pair of ex-LMS locos in GWR territory on 17 March 1968. No 42968, closest to the camera, was new from Crewe Works on 24 January 1934, as No 13268, allocated to 1A (Willesden). Renumbered by the LMS to 2968 on 20 September 1935, it became No 42968 post-nationalisation on 18 December 1948. It was spared the acetylene cutter after withdrawal on 31 December 1966, being speedily despatched to Barry by March 1967 and rescued by the Severn Valley Railway in December 1973. No 47298 beyond was designed for slightly lighter freight duties, and was ten years older when withdrawn in 1966. Barry welcomed it in 1967, until departure to the Llangollen Railway in 1974.

Right **NEWPORT** Through the keyhole! What remains of No 92050, new in September 1955, is viewed through the cab roof of another loco at United Wagon scrapyard on 17 March 1968. It had been withdrawn from Aintree shed just six months earlier. *All MJS*

Above: **NEWPORT** We are back at J. Cashmore's yard on 17 March 1968, craning over the boundary wall to snatch a portrait of Nos 34036 *Westward Ho!*, 34052 *Lord Dowding* and 44835. The two 4-6-2s, fresh in 1936 from Brighton Works, were withdrawn in July 1967, at the end of steam on the Southern Region, while the 'Black 5', eight years younger, succumbed a month later. Although relatively recent arrivals at the yard, the wheels are rapidly rusting in the local sea air. Note how discarded items are dumped adjacent to new deliveries. *MJS*

Right: **SPRING VALE** On 27 April 1968 Nos 73050 and 73069, both allocated to 9H (Patricroft), swing round the curve at Spring Vale with 1Z77, the Manchester Rail Travel Society/Severn Valley Railway Society 'North West Tour' working between Stalybridge and Bolton. Note the different tender styles. *MJS collection*

Right: **LOCATION UNKNOWN** On 20 April 1968 No 48773 heads the Manchester Rail Travel Society/Severn Valley Railway Society 'North West Tour', from Bolton to Stockport. *MJS collection*

Right: **CARNFORTH** is seen on 15 April 1968 Another aspect of No 75048. Note how the post-nationalisation, BR-generated locos were endowed with the much higher running plates, to give much clearer and easier access to the motion, both for routine and remedial actions.

Below right: **CARNFORTH** Compared to many of its companions in the yard, No 92223 was a spring chicken, being new less than ten years earlier, on 14 June 1958. While looking the part, with coal in the tender as if waiting for the next duty, it has already been graced with a 'hand-made' front number plate and was, indeed, withdrawn just five days after this view. The final end came at Arnott, Young at the company's Parkgate & Rawmarsh depot on 18 September 1968. In slightly happier times, it served as a banker at Bromsgrove for the Lickey Incline in October 1963, but had sustained damage to its cylinders by the year end! Initially withdrawn on 22 February 1964, it was reinstated three months later. *All MJS*

Below **CARNFORTH**. One of the few ex-LMS sheds to survive until the end of steam on BR, it closed to steam on 5 August 1968, by which time it was a Mecca for enthusiasts. Representing three generations of motive power, No 75048 (right) is in conversation with No 45394, in company with one of the new breed, a Type 2 diesel. The two steamers, new in October 1953 from Swindon Works and August 1937 from Armstrong Whitworth respectively, were both well-travelled over the WCML in their BR service.

Right and below: **CARNFORTH** is seen again on 15 April 1968. No 45342 comes into the picture at the end of a hard day's work. Note how the cleaner has attempted a pre-BR persona, with just the last four numbers clearly visible. Built by Armstrong Whitworth in April 1937, the loco was housed at Leicester Midland (15C) shed at nationalisation and was an MML loco until 3 July 1965, when it was transferred to pastures new, many miles north on the WCML at Carnforth. BR renumbering came in January 1950, later than many. It survived to the very end of steam.

Right: **LOSTOCK HALL** was, later in the day, a required port of call on our way home. On the left is No 44713, completed by BR on 6 November 1948 to the standard 'Black 5' LMS design. It served six different BR sheds, on the southern half of the WCML, beginning at Crewe North as new, before transfer north to Lostock Hall on 24 June 1967 and withdrawal at the end of steam, although the official date has been recorded as 7 September 1968. It was subsequently cut at Draper's yard in Hull. *All MJS*

Above: **GUILDFORD** Steam on the Southern Region had finished in 1967, so to see a steam locomotive passing through Guildford was unusual to say the least! BR Swindon-built Class 9F 2-10-0 No 92203 had been purchased by the well-known and respected artist David Shepherd, and he had arranged for it to be transferred under its own steam from Speke Junction to the Longmoor Military Railway in Hampshire. It is seen here en route on 7 April 1968.
Ray Ruffell/Slip Coach PS Ltd Archive

Left and right: **LOSTOCK HALL** Two angles on No 48646 on 15 April 1968. Left is the view you would see moments before being run over (!), and No D3846 has contrived to sneak into the picture. On the right it heads the row outside the shed building, with Nos 48476 and 48492 immediately behind. They were, respectively, new from Brighton Works in November 1943, Swindon Works in June 1945 and Horwich Works in July 1945. Of the trio, only No 48492 had already been withdrawn, with the others lasting until the very end of steam. Note the perfunctory stop arrangement of a single lamp atop a spare sleeper! *Both MJS*

Above: **UNKNOWN LOCATION** Exerting effort with its long train, No 92218 hauls at the Manchester Rail Travel Society / Severn Valley Railway Society 'North West Tour' at Stockport, en route to Liverpool Lime Street on 27 April 1968, having picked up the train at Edgeley Junction.
Ken Horan, Peter Skelton collection

Above: **CONSETT** One of a class of originally 201 engines, 65033 new from Gateshead Works in March 1889, as NER 876 and renumbered by BR in December 1948, was the last of the class to survive. Initially, withdrawn on 22 November 1939, it was re-instated in January 1940 and rebuilt with a '67A' boiler in 1943. It became the last of class over Stainmore Summit, on a RCTS tour of 7 May 1960, and last of the class, finally withdrawn in April 1962. It is seen here at Consett in April 1968. Thankfully, preservation followed - at the Tanfield Rly in 1970. At the time of writing, it was in the hands of those keen to see the loco work again. *G S Hearse*

Right: **LOCATION UNKNOWN** While not knowing where the train was captured is a disappointment, the image is still full of features to savour. The separate line to the left, the electricity pylons, telegraph posts, semaphore signals, a myriad of lines, smoke from the chimney, full coal wagons and the industrial scene behind collectively encapsulate what appealed to the steam enthusiast in those heady days in the 1960s. Unfortunately looking rather careworn, with just a badly chalked/painted front number but a discernible 8C (Speke Junction) allocation, No 45386 will, however, be another to battle to the end. New from Armstrong Whitworth in July 1937, it was at Barrow by 1948 (gaining its BR number by July of that year) and Lostock Hall by the time of withdrawal on the last day of steam. *MJS*

Left: **ROSE GROVE** Another loco without a front number plate, and therefore unidentified, a 9F 2-10-0 heads a Saturdays-only parcels working near Rose Grove on 4 May 1968, with the engine shed coaling tower in the distance. With the engine blowing off, it could be that it is being held at the colour light signal. The clean ballast indicates recent attention from the engineers. *MJS collection*

WIGSTON GLEN PARVA On a sunny 5 May 1968 what appears to be a three-car Cravens-built Class 105 DMU enters the station with the Sundays-only 15.10 Leicester-Birmingham local service. The train could be stopping here, despite there being an absence of waiting passengers, but not today, as this facility had closed just two months earlier on 4 March, which was the date that such local services were withdrawn from the Birmingham (New Street)-Leicester (London Road) route via Nuneaton Abbey Street. Note that the all-over-yellow front end has replaced the original 'whiskers'. A delightful image of what would soon disappear. *Mike Mitchell, MJS collection*

Right: **HEATON MERSEY** Situated on the south side of the fork of the Cheadle and Didsbury lines, west of Tiviot Dale station, this Cheshire eight-row straight shed was opened in January 1889. It saw virtually no change thereafter, except for a new roof and a 70-foot turntable (replacing the previous 50-foot version) in 1952. Allocated code 9F by BR in 1948, it came under the jurisdiction of Longsight (Manchester). Closure came on 6 May 1968 and the shed is seen shortly after, looking out towards the shed yard, with abandoned LMS motive power and a 'Standard' 9F 2-10-0 in view. *MJS collection*

Above left and left: **POTTERS BAR** 1968 was the 50th Anniversary of the first non-stop run from King's Cross to Edinburgh. The train, known from 1924 as the 'Flying Scotsman', had left King's Cross at 10.00am hauled by LNER 'A3' 'Pacific' No 4472 *Flying Scotsman*. In 1968 *Flying Scotsman*, BR No 60103, was owned by businessman Alan Pegler, so to celebrate the event he planned to repeat the performance on 1 May. On the day *Flying Scotsman* was back at King's Cross with its special train, while on an adjacent platform stood the daily 'Flying Scotsman' behind 'Deltic' Type 5 diesel-electric No 9021 *Argyll and Sutherland Highlander* (later No 55021). Both trains were due to depart at the traditional time of 10.00am.

Although the steam engine was allowed to precede No 9021 out of the terminus, by the time the 'Deltic' approached Potters Bar Tunnel it was well ahead, and some 10 minutes elapsed before *Flying Scotsman* appeared, as seen in the second picture. A non-stop run was only possible due to the 'Pacific' being fitted with a second, water-carrying tender. The train just made it to Edinburgh without a stop, although at one point it had to slow down to a walking pace. *Both Phil Horton*

NEAR NANTYRONEN Many thousands of tourists and holidaymakers have travelled on and enjoyed the delights of the Vale of Rheidol Railway in mid-Wales, but how many realise that the locos on the line were the last BR steam? Whereas most consider 4 August 1968 to have been the end, the three narrow-gauge engines on the VoR were owned and operated by British Rail until April 1989, when the line was sold to the Brecon Mountain Railway. The youngest of the trio, No 9 *Prince of Wales*, was new in 1924 as GWR No 1213, although officially known as a rebuild of an earlier loco of the same name. It was renumbered 9 in March 1949 and named in June 1956, when its sisters also received identities.

Above: **HOLT** railway station was opened in 1887, served by the Midland & Great Northern Joint Railway. Most of the M&GNJR was closed by British Railways in 1959, but a short section, from Melton Constable station via Holt to Sheringham (services continuing on to Cromer and Norwich) escaped closure for a few more years, finally succumbing in 1964, when the branch was cut back to Sheringham (now the nearest national network railhead, served by frequent services to Norwich along the 'Bittern Line'). In 1965, within a year of the closure of this line, the North Norfolk Railway was formed to restore part of the line as an independent heritage steam railway. Initially it operated between Sheringham and Weybourne; later it was extended to the eastern edge of Holt. The original station, here in near-derelict condition, is seen on 20 June 1968.

Right: **MELTON CONSTABLE** Decorative supports for the platform canopy are seen on 20 June 1968. *All MJS collection*

Three views of **SHERINGHAM** on 20 June 1968.

Right: A decidedly wet vista, in the early days of restoration, shows a selection of motive power waiting for a return to work. Head of the line are two Maschinenbau single-unit vehicles, originally supplied to BR in April 1958 and intended to be the answer for reducing operating costs on lightly used lines.

Behind them are two survivors of ex-GER vintage. No 61572, new from Beyer Peacock on 24 August 1928 as LNER No 8572, was renumbered 1572 on 16 June 1946 and withdrawn from Norwich on 20 September 1961. No 65462 was new as GER No 564 in 1912, becoming LNER 7564, then 5462 in 1946. Its brush with death came in October 1962, when released from service at Stratford shed. *Below:* A close-up of No 65462, looking in fine form and ready for its public. *Below right:* Sheringham East signal box, located at the end of the platform, is see during a moment of sunshine after the rain. *All MJS collection*

Right: **SHERINGHAM** A close-up of No 61572, not looking quite as ready as its companions on 20 June 1968. A roughly draped tarpaulin serves to protect the main part of the boiler. Following eventual full restoration, the loco has given excitement and pleasure to many hundreds riding between here and Holt, at the other end of the North Norfolk Railway.

Right: **SWAFFHAM** Also captured on 20 June 1968, a Swaffham lamp and totem stand proudly in the GER colours. Situated east of Narborough & Pentney station on the GER's Lynn & Dereham Railway, it opened on 10 August 1847, closed to freight in 1966 and to passengers on 9 September 1968 – hence the cleanliness of the sign, as the station was still open when seen.

Left: **LOCATION UNKNOWN** On 23 June 1968 No 48033 is adorned with a garish headboard, announcing the train as being the LCGB (NW Branch) 'Two Cities Limited' rail tour. Originating at 10.50 from Liverpool Lime Street, the 8F took it to Earlestown, via Manchester Victoria, then resumed power later at Manchester Victoria to return the special to Liverpool, where it arrived 1 hour 36 minutes late! Note the photographer crouching down by the gradient post, left of centre!
All MJS collection

ROSE GROVE A classic front-end portrait, in the shed yard in June 1968, shows No 48278 in company with No 75019. The former is adorned with 10F, the shed's final BR code, while the 'Standard 4' 4-6-0 wears 10A, denoting Carnforth as its home. Originally No WD565 when new from the North British Locomotive Co in June 1942, the 8F became No 8278 for the LMS in December 1943, and 48278 for BR in August 1952, 4½ years after nationalisation, being one of the latest locos to receive its new persona. By comparison, No 75019 was not born until March 1952, at Swindon Works, and lived only 16 years to its end in August 1968. It had the distinction of working the last steam freight on BR, 6P52, the 14.55 Heysham-Carnforth goods on 3 August 1968.

ROSE GROVE More front ends on that day in June 1968, but this time seen across the shed yard. From left to right are Nos 44899, an unidentified 'Black 5', and our two friends Nos 48278 and 75019. '4899' was new from Crewe Works in September 1945, and was renumbered for BR in August 1949. Until its move to Rose Grove in January 1968, it had spent the whole of its BR life as a servant of Carlisle (Kingmoor) shed. *All MJS collectionAbove:*

ABERYSTWYTH No 9 *Prince of Wales* is about to depart from the seaside terminus on 3 June.

Below: **DEVIL'S BRIDGE** Here we see No 9 *Prince of Wales* at the other end of this scenic narrow-gauge route

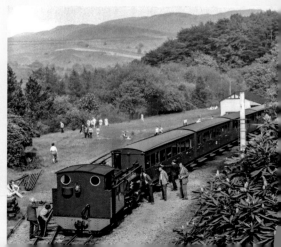

Left: **KENDAL** Seen from a passing DMU between Windermere and Oxenholme, a 'Black 5' shunts the yard at Kendal on 24 July 1968. At Windermere the turntable was in the process of being broken up, so the engine of the daily pick-up goods would have had to run tender-first from Carnforth. *Phil Horton*

Above right: **ASHCHURCH FOR TEWKESBURY** Due to the vagaries of fate, Ashchurch, once a tiny village some 2 miles east of Tewkesbury, became an important location on the railway map, with an attractive and impressive building to boot. By 24 July 1968, however, its fortunes had changed dramatically and it was near closure; apart from the clutch of spotters on the left, No D1818 would be storming south through the station with its freight receiving virtually no attention apart from the signaller in the box on the right. The left-hand branch once ran to Great Malvern and the right-hand one to Birmingham via Evesham and Redditch. Closed in 1971, a new facility was opened in 1997. The only remains in the 21st century, apart from the dead straight tracks, are the warehouse on the left (without the top storey), the wall on which the boys sit, the brick building next to them (now a Network Rail office), the tall tree (much bigger), and the former Evesham line, now serving the local MoD Camp.

Left: **ASHCHURCH FOR TEWKESBURY** The view looking south on 24 July 1968 shows more of the wonderful architecture and the impressive tree. *Both Robin Leleux, MJS collection*

Left: **ASHCHURCH FOR TEWKESBURY** Happy days on 24 July 1968 – the station is still open, the semaphore stands proud, gas lamps wait for the evening, and express trains had 10-12 coaches. Only a steam engine is missing to complete the picture! No D29, new from Derby Works in May 1961 and later to become No 45002 under TOPS in June 1973, speeds south through the station with an inter-regional working.

Below left: **BARRY DOCKS** The one and only, literally. The sole BR 8P 4-6-2, No 71000 *Duke of Gloucester*, does not show itself to distinction, wallowing in the weeds, also on 24 July 1968. With a cylinder destroyed, it was considered a preservation project too far, but where there is a will there is a way, and enthusiasts, not least at the GCR in the early 1970s, saw to it that the loco lived again and has once more seen express duties on the main line

Below: **LYDNEY JUNCTION** No, the 'Hymek' is not about to smash through the closed crossing gates! No D7006 is involved with infrastructure work on Saturday 27 July 1968 and the driver looks back along the platform as he awaits further instructions. The 'Hymeks' were considered by many to be among the most aesthetic of diesels, introduced from 1961; No D7006 appeared in October of that year, but was to fall foul of BR's antipathy to hydraulic transmission, being withdrawn in unseemly haste in September 1971. *All Robin Leleux, MJS collection*

So we arrive at August 1968, the month that it was all supposed to come to an end, the very last days of standard-gauge steam-hauled trains on British Rail. The last hurrah was to be a £15 15s 0d special on 11 August 1968.

Left: **BOLTON** Peter Simmonds stands, hands on hips, aghast and bewildered at the state of No 44829 in Bolton shed yard on 2 August 1968 – a smokebox at one end and a tender at the other, and precious little in between. New from Crewe Works in August 1944 and recipient of its BR number soon after nationalisation, in October 1948, it spent most of its BR life between sheds in the Birmingham area, Holyhead, Crewe and Northampton, before decamping north to Workington for nine months from April 1967. Returning south to Bolton on 6 January 1968, it was withdrawn four months later, before the ignominy seen here.

Below right: **BOLTON** Looks can be deceptive! Despite being just two days before the end of steam on BR, everything appears normal in the shed yard and No 44947 looks relatively smart in its lined livery, despite being out of service, having been withdrawn two months earlier. Its build plate would say Horwich Works, from where it emerged in February 1946. To the left stands diminutive diesel shunter No D2227, new as No 11133 from the Vulcan Foundry in November 1955. It began life as an ER loco, at Stratford shed. After just short of ten years there, it made its only move, to Bolton, on 18 July 1964. It was also withdrawn when seen here, but four months earlier! *Both MJS*

Right: **BOLTON** A lone spotter breaks one of the cardinal railway rules, not to step on the rails, rather to step over them to avoid slipping and injury. Whether he is interested in No 48319 or wishes to reach the main line to see what arrives past the cleared semaphore signal on 2 August 1968 is unknown. Built at Crewe Works in January 1944, No 48319's BR number was applied in June 1948. The end came exactly 20 years later and, like the others in the yard, it is already out of commission. It was well-travelled in BR service, being allocated to 11 different sheds, mostly on the MML before transfer to the WCML at Fleetwood in November 1963. *(see also title page)*

Left: **BOLTON** Inside, the status of the locos is no better, with both No 48702, on the left, and its anagram No 48720 both dead when seen on 2 August. Both were built at Brighton Works, in May and August 1944 respectively, but No 48720 was initially allocated to the LNER as No 7666. It became No 3115 on 28 April 1946 and 3515 on 7 March 1947, before a transfer to the LMS seven months later, on 16 October, just in time for nationalisation. Its first allocation had been to Mexborough.

Right: **WIGAN SPRINGS BRANCH** Still on 2 August 1968, we have reached a depot with live locos, albeit diesels! One of the brand-new breed, English Electric Type 4 No D421 *Rodney*, less than four months old, stands outside the shed building next to Type 2 No D7548, three years old but certainly less powerful. They both had similar life spans, being withdrawn in 1990 and 1986 respectively. *All MJS*

Three at **PATRICROFT** on 2 August 1968.

Above left: Peter and I spent the first weekend of August 1968 chasing steam in the North West. Here he is, capturing 'the perfect angle' of No 48390, gaily adorned with a renumbering to 70036 (why?), named *Earl of Ducie* and with the legends 'Patricroft Flyer', 'The End' and 'V (for victory?) to Steam'. Sadly, there would be no more flying for this loco as it had been withdrawn three months earlier. No 73143, to the right, built in December 1956 and new to Leicester Midland shed, is also dead, having been withdrawn on 13 July 1968. It was wholly a MML loco until transfer to Patricroft in February 1964. Note the very smart spotter's outfit!

Above right: Holes in the shed roof let in shafts of light that were a distinct challenge to a camera! No 48467, with painted front number and a 9H shedplate, was new from Swindon Works in March 1945, received its BR number in October 1948, and saw withdrawal on 13 July 1968. It was another long-term incumbent of the MML, until a switch to the North West and Liverpool in June 1966. Such were the mass withdrawals that year that many locos were left mouldering in an intact state for months before release to the scrap merchant.

Left: Another view of No 73143, with the rust betraying abandonment to the elements. *All MJS*

Above: **PATRICROFT** One of a number of 'Standard 5'
4-6-0s dead on shed on 2 August 1968, No 73138 had been new
to Holyhead in December 1956. Moving to Leicester Midland
within weeks saw it become another MML loco, until the final
move to the North West at Patricroft on 6 June 1964.
The end had come 2½ weeks prior to this view.

Above right: **PATRICROFT** You could have spent a week in this
shed and still found new angles, including this one of No 48374 on
2 August 1968. It was a Wellingborough possession for the whole
of its BR career up to 10 July 1965, when it moved to Northwich.
Brief stays at Speke Junction and Edge Hill finally saw it at
Patricroft, on 11 May 1968. Its death knell was two months later.

Right: **CARNFORTH** Nos 45231 (left) and 45342 are both still
alive and fighting a rearguard action on 3 August 1968, receiving
attention under the towers, ready for their next move. No hi-vis
gear in those days! *All MJS*

Two tower portraits at
CARNFORTH on 3 August 1968.

Left: Featuring No 45231, this
view highlights so much of the
appeal of the old railway and,
more specifically, engine sheds —
the mighty tower, telegraph pole
complete with access ladder and
somewhat unusual rudimentary
rails to guide the ash tubs, yet still
ash in the pit. New from Armstrong
Whitworth in August 1936, this
loco meandered through a variety
of smaller sheds until finally ending
up at Carnforth on 11 May 1968.
Happily, it avoided the trip to the
cutter's yard to find preservation
at the East Lancashire Railway,
where it was named *The Sherwood
Forester. Right:* By comparison with
the workworn appearance of No
45231, No 45342 is a credit to
the Carnforth shedmaster, clean
and complete with the shed code
on the front buffer beam. Full of
steam during refuelling, it is fighting
to the end against the presence of
the diesels left and right. Another
product of Armstrong Whitworth,
this time in April 1937, it was a
Leicester Midland shed resident
by nationalisation and remained
an MML loco, even moving to
Leicester Central shed for
18 months from 12 January 1963,
until the last move, to Carnforth,
on 3 July 1965. *Both MJS*

Right: **CARNFORTH** We have already seen No 45342 under the tower in Carnforth shed yard on 3 August 1968. Moments later it has been moved to the rear of the shed, its last operational movement. Earlier in the day it had powered the very last steam working from Barrow, 8P76, the 09.30 goods to Carnforth. It then adjourned to the shed. This view shows its very last moments, parked in the siding alongside No 75020 and left to die – a rare record of an actual withdrawal. The fireman, having completed his final duty on the locomotive, walks to join his colleagues, who have gathered to witness the event. *MJS*

We now move to **LOSTOCK HALL** on 3 August 1968.

Right: Two spotters are unaware that they are on film, as they, like me, tour the shed during its last throes. Left to right are Nos 45305, a well-travelled loco on the WCML, complete with freshly painted buffers, which will go on to preservation; 45212, also preserved, after being the last BR steam loco shunting at Preston the following day; 48476, the last 8F in BR service on 4 August, then scrapped at T. W. Ward in October 1968; D5280, scrapped at Swindon Works in January 1987; and D7633, later preserved on the Severn Valley Railway. *Above right:* A small throng gathers to capture the locos on shed, including three 'Black 5s': Nos 44894, which served ten different sheds during its BR career, ending at Carnforth on 10 July 1965; 45305, to be preserved; and 45407 (right), also to see preserved life.

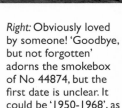

Right: Obviously loved by someone! 'Goodbye, but not forgotten' adorns the smokebox of No 44874, but the first date is unclear. It could be '1950-1968', as the loco was shedded at Preston in the earlier year, which would tie in with '24K', which was the final code of that shed until it closed in 1961. So, presumably, the engine was fondly remembered by a railman. *All MJS*

Three at **ROSE GROVE** on 3 August 1968.

Right: Looking in fine external condition, apart from much, largely undecipherable, graffiti on engine and tender, and some form of decoration tied to the smokebox door handle, No 45156 stands in the shed yard waiting the next turn. New from Armstrong Whitworth in July 1935, Works No 1197, it was graced with an *Ayrshire Yeomanry* nameplate from 19 September 1936, one of four 'Black 5s' named after Scottish military in 1936/37. Its first allocation was St Rollox (Glasgow), and it stayed there until a move south to Newton Heath (Manchester) on 20 April 1957. After withdrawal the day after this view, it was rapidly despatched at T. W. Ward's Beighton scrapyard in November. Note that it is without its nameplate here.

Right: Still in steam at this point, No 48393 will not move far before its end tomorrow! It was new from Horwich Works in April 1945 and was another MML worker until a move to the North West in November 1966.

Left: A quartet of 8Fs, including Nos 48448 and 48278. A symptom of the increasing abandonment of locos, the former pathway is now covered by small mountains of ash and coal, which would satisfy many households! More graffiti adorns No 48278, announcing it to be 'Last steam Copy Pit banker. August 3 1968'. *All MJS*

Right: **ROSE GROVE** is deceptively busy, though occupied by dead locos, with the exception No 48773, which is very much alive. Built by the North British Locomotive Co in December 1940 for the War Effort, it was originally allocated the LMS number 8233, but this changed to WD307 as it was earmarked for overseas duties. It was duly sent to Persia in September 1941, where it stayed until its return to the UK in 1952. It was finally bought by BR in July 1957 and allocated the next available 8F number. Happily, it went on to preservation.

Right: **LOSTOCK HALL** No 48493 stands in a prominent position on 4 August 1968, along with Nos 45305 and 45212, which we have already seen. No 48476 is also visible, the final BR 8F, which again we have already seen. Working from Staveley for its BR life until November 1962, No 48493 moved to the southern half of the WCML. While it is helpful to have the number on the smokebox, the painted numerals could have been more aesthetic! *Both MJS*

On the final day, 4 August 1968, at or near **LOSTOCK HALL**.

Above left: Amazing what spit and polish will achieve! The nameplate and front end of No 70013 *Oliver Cromwell* could hardly have looked better when first out of the shops, thanks to the time and enthusiasm of local supporters and railmen. On shed preparing for the final steam runs on BR, it is hardly surprising that it and No 45110, on the left, will be saved for preservation.

Above: Having retired to the countryside, for lunch and to snap whatever came by, all Peter and I saw was No 45407 scuttling along the main line. Where it was going and what to do we were and are still blissfully unaware.

Left: Another view of *Oliver Cromwell* before we left the shed for the last time. Last-minute remedial repairs are in process (possibly to tighten the nameplate securing nuts?) and all is witnessed by a noticeably young girl and her father. One wonders where she is now, some 50-plus years later! *All MJS*

On the main line, close to **ROSE GROVE** shed on 4 August 1968

.Left: We have already seen No 48773, the only live steam on shed, and this is the same engine from another view. Oh, happy days, as the sun has brought out the white shirts and cameras in this pre-Health & Safety era! Hordes of ferroequinologist ants capture their shot of the loco before returning to await the arrival of 1Z74, the Locomotive Club of Great Britain 'Farewell to Steam Rail Tour', which was 45 minutes late at this stage.

Left: More ants, at the same place, same date, but a different tour. Nos 44871 and 44894 pause for their portraits at the head of 1Z78, the Stephenson Locomotive Society (Midland Area) 'Farewell to Steam No 1' tour. Kodak, Ilford, Fuji and the like must have been making a fortune on that day! The tour began and ended with No E3093 from Birmingham (New Street) to Stockport, with No D7588 also taking part between Stockport and Manchester Victoria before this pair of 'Black 5s' took over. *Both Gerald Adams, MJS collection*

Three more views of 1Z78, the Stephenson Locomotive Society (Midland Area) 'Farewell to Steam No 1' rail tour at **ROSE GROVE** on 4 August 1968.

Above: A rear portrait of both the train engine and the pilot. *Above right:* A portrait of No 44871 as the pilot.

Right: A portrait of No 44894 as the train engine.
All Gerald Adams, MJS collection

Below: **NEAR SHREWSBURY** Towards the end of BR steam lines of steam engines could be seen en route to one of the country's many scrapyards. Here a line of seven Stanier 8F 2-8-0s await their final journey in sidings south of Shrewsbury on Friday 10 August. The engines were photographed from a passing Llanelly to Shrewsbury DMU. *Phil Horton*

Above: **ROSE GROVE** Back inside the shed confines, No 44899 stands by the turntable. This must have a been a rare 'cop' for local spotters, as the loco served Carlisle (Kingmoor) shed for all of its BR life until January 1968, when it found its way to this shed for seven short months. Having normal-sized numbers, it had obviously not been into Cowlairs Works for attention. No 48423 can be seen outside the main shed on its last official day of its life, after a wandering existence up and down the southern half of the WCML until June 1965. *Gerald Adams, MJS collection*

Three more from **ROSE GROVE** on 4 August 1968.

Above: Another view of No 48278, seen before with the 'Last steam Copy Pit banker. August 3 1968' graffiti, but this time a day later.

Above: With yet more fond messages, this time on its tender, No 45397 stands trapped among other withdrawn locos. Another product of Armstrong Whitworth, this time from August 1937, it received its BR number in May 1948, when it was stationed at Aston (Birmingham) shed. Carlisle Kingmoor, Blackpool and Fleetwood followed before a final residence at Rose Grove.

Left: An unidentified 8F has its smokebox identity hidden behind '70013 would you believe?' No, we wouldn't – nor that it was named *Old Harry*! Note the spare connecting rod on the frame. 1944-vintage, Brighton-built No 48666 stands next to it. *All Gerald Adams, MJS collection*

Four more at or near to **ROSE GROVE** on 4 August 1968

.Left: No 48393 has already been seen on shed earlier, but the day before, when it was still in steam. That has now died and it does not even attract attention from the spotters at either end! Some kind soul has attempted to grace it with 'LMS' ownership, but others have had other ideas.

Top right: The little girl appears again with her white shoes now probably nearer grey. No 48400 is here joined by No 48727, new from Brighton Works on 15 September 1944 for the LNER as No 7673. Renumbered 3122 on 19 May 1946 and 3522 on 20 March 1947, it was transferred to the LMS on 8 November 1947, going to Newton Heath. Fourteen different sheds then followed until final transfer to Rose Grove on 9 March 1968. It hauled the last steam freight on 3 August 1968 from Blackburn to Preston.

Above: Another portrait of one of the locos on shed. No 48400 looks in good shape and presentable apart from the semi-obliterated graffiti. The first of the class built at Swindon Works, in June 1943, its first allocation was St Philips Marsh (Bristol). A move to Crewe North had come by 1946, and it then led a nomadic life, being at Toton, Swansea Victoria and Llanelly, then to sheds in the North West from September 1964. I wonder what the little girl thought of all the dust, ash, etc. threatening her white clothes!

Right: We are now leaving Rose Grove and heading for Carnforth, via Hellifield, aboard 1Z78, the Stephenson Locomotive Society (Midland Area) 'Farewell to Steam No 1' rail tour, behind Nos 44871 and 44894.
All Gerald Adams, MJS collection

Above: **LOCATION UNKNOWN** Steam locomotives are thirsty animals and Nos 44871 and 44894 are no exception, as 1Z78, the Stephenson Locomotive Society (Midland Area) 'Farewell to Steam No 1' rail tour pauses for a drinks interval, under the watchful eyes of the crew.
Gerald Adams, MJS collection

Above: **PRESTON** The headboard says it all. On the penultimate day of normal steam on BR, 3 August 1968, No 45318 stands under the lights at Preston station with the final scheduled passenger train on BR – the 21.25 to Liverpool Exchange. A coffin was carried onto the train by steam fans, who also collected autographs from the engine crews. Lasting to the very end of steam, finally allocated to Lostock Hall shed, No 45318 was not formally withdrawn until 7 September 1968. *Peter Skelton*

Overleaf: **MANCHESTER VICTORIA** All polished for the occasion on the last day of steam at Manchester Victoria, Nos 73069 and 48476 await their next move on 4 August 1968 with the Railway Correspondence & Travel Society's 'End of Steam Commemorative Rail Tour', which they will haul to Blackburn. Twenty-one-year-old fireman Jim Marlor is seen leaning from No 73069's cab, as it moves forward with the 8F prior to being attached to the train. *Peter Skelton*

Above: **LIVERPOOL LIME STREET** Prior to its departure at 09.10, 'Black 5' No 45110 awaits its passengers with BR's 'Fifteen Guinea Special' at Liverpool (Lime Street) on 11 August 1968. *Phil Horton*

Above: **PATRICROFT** One week after the tumultuous weekend, No 73069 stands ready for work if needed on 11 August 1968. The low angle highlights the high running plate of the two 'Standard 5s', and the steam effect would seem to indicate a slow shutter speed. *Peter Skelton collection*

Right: **PARKSIDE** Between Liverpool (Lime Street) and Manchester (Victoria) the train was scheduled to make two stops. The first was at Rainhill, the location of the Liverpool & Manchester Railway's trials of rival steam engines in October 1829, the 150th Anniversary of which was famously celebrated in 1979. The second was at the site of Parkside station, where the MP William Huskisson became the first railway-related death deemed worthy of wide-scale reporting; he was run over by Stephenson's *Rocket* at the railway's opening on 15 September 1830. The scene at Parkside on 11 August 1968 appears to be another case of mass trespass, although it was officially sanctioned as can be seen from the ladders that allowed passengers to reach the trackbed. *Phil Horton*

Left: **PATRICROFT** The final countdown! No 45110 runs past a signal box at Patricroft, at the head of British Rail's 'Fifteen Guinea Special' on 11 August 1968. Five minutes late at this point, after time lost at Huyton earlier, the 'Black 5' is near the end of its outward journey, when it will hand over to *Oliver Cromwell* at Manchester Victoria. *Ken Horan, Peter Skelton collection*

Bottom left: **BLACKBURN** The 'Fifteen Guinea Special' was taken forward from Manchester (Victoria) by BR 'Britannia' 'Pacific' No 70013 *Oliver Cromwell*. After an on-time departure at 11.06, an 8-minute stop was scheduled at Blackburn to take on water. Clearly whoever devised the 'Special' schedule did not know how long it takes to water a steam engine, or that the water crane at the north end of the platform had been disconnected. The engine therefore had to be taken off the train to run to the water crane at the opposite end of the station. Fortunately, as seen here, water was available, otherwise the 'Special' would have terminated prematurely. It finally left some 30 minutes late. *Phil Horton*

L & NW, L & Y and MID. Rlys.

Available on the DATE of issue ONLY

11 AUG 1968

LIVERPOOL/MANCHESTER

TO

CARLISLE

and back

6145

Via Weaste *‖*, The Oaks *‖*, Wilpshire for Ribchester *‖*, Kirkby Stephen & Ravenstonedale *‖* Closed

By the 9.10 o'clock morning train from the Lime Street Station Liverpool 11.6 o'clock morning train from the Victoria Station, Manchester

THE LAST JOURNEY ON STANDARD GAUGE OF ANY STEAM TRAIN OWNED BY BRITISH RAIL

315s Covered Carriages **315s [SEE BACK**

Right: **AIS GILL** Still running 30 minutes late, No 70013 *Oliver Cromwell* takes water with the 'Fifteen Guinea Special' at Ais Gill, between Ribblehead and Carlisle, surrounded by its passengers and other bystanders. According to the schedule, 5 minutes were allowed to take water at Blea Moor, but in the event Ais Gill was used instead, where 20 minutes had been allowed for passengers to admire the scenery! In fact only 14 minutes was taken, although the special still arrived at Carlisle over half an hour late. *Phil Horton*

APPROACHING CARLISLE on the line from Ribblehead, the 'Fifteen Guinea Special' is over half an hour late as it passes 'Black 5' Nos 44871 and 44781, which are due to haul the train back to Manchester Victoria. Bystanders are clearly not welcome as the engines are guarded by three uniformed railway policemen. *Phil Horton*

CARLISLE Its job done, 'Britannia' 'Pacific' No 70013 *Oliver Cromwell* stands at Carlisle (Citadel) after arrival with the 'Fifteen Guinea Special'. The engine later ran under its own steam via Norwich to Diss where, on 17 August, it was taken by road to Bressingham Gardens. The engine has since been restored to main-line running and is currently based on the heritage Great Central Railway at Loughborough. *Phil Horton*

Above: **BLEA MOOR** Leaving Carlisle 15 minutes late ,'Black 5' Nos 44871 and 44781 were worked hard and arrived at Blea Moor, where they are pictured, only a minute late. Here 6 minutes had been allowed to water two engines! The train was therefore back to square one, leaving Blea Moor 15 minutes late once more. A further water stop was made at Blackburn, at the correct water crane, and the train arrived at Manchester Victoria only 12 minutes late. No 44871 was subsequently preserved and has recently seen action on the 'Jacobite' train between Fort William and Mallaig. No 44781 was used in the making of the film *The Virgin Soldiers* ; disguised as a Malayan engine, it was deliberately derailed and, after filming, was broken up on site.

Right: **MANCHESTER EXCHANGE** As the 'Black 5'-hauled 'Fifteen Guinea Special' arrives back at Manchester Victoria it passes sister engine No 45110 outside Manchester Exchange; No 45110 will shortly back onto the rear of the 'Special' to haul it back to Liverpool (Lime Street). This was the very last standard-gauge BR steam engine to work a train. The engine was subsequently preserved and has for many years been based on the Severn Valley Railway at Bridgnorth. It is not currently serviceable. *Both Phil Horton*

September

Left: **BELGRAVE & BIRSTALL** Opened by the Great Central Railway in 1899, this station served the then villages of Belgrave and Birstall in Leicestershire. It had a typical GCR island layout, with tracks on either side of the platform, and, despite offering a fair service between Leicester and Nottingham, it was overtaken by progress and the rise of the car and closed, with all other local stations on the line, on 4 March 1963. In September 1968 the line is still open and the station furniture looks in remarkable condition. Sadly, after the line's closure in 1969, vandals had a field day here, meaning that the station could not be reopened when the new GCR preservation movement was gathering pace. This is now the site of Leicester North station. My grandfather's allotment was just behind me to the right – ideal for spotting! *MJS*

Bottom left: **RUGBY TESTING STATION** was a railway testing plant in Rugby, Warwickshire. Originally the vision of Sir Nigel Gresley as a joint LMS-LNER operation, construction was started in the late 1930s, but then delayed by the war. It was eventually opened in 1948. The engine featured was built in December 1951 by Metro-Vickers as gas turbine locomotive No 18100; it was converted in January 1958 to an electric as No E1000, then E2001 in 1958/59. It is seen at the plant five months after it was withdrawn in April 1968; its first number can still be seen on the side. *P. H. Groom, MJS collection*

Below: **TENBY** A Class 120 DMU arrives at Tenby forming a Pembroke Dock to Whitland service on 11 September 1968. Until September 1963 many of these workings would have consisted of through coaches to Paddington, attached at Whitland and hauled by an ex-GWR 'Small Prairie'. Note that semaphore signals are still in use on the branch. *Phil Horton*

Right: **PELAW** On 7 September 1968 at Pelaw, Gateshead, alongside a large Co-operative Wholesale Society Ltd building, this interesting view of preserved 'A3' 4-6-2 No 4472 *Flying Scotsman* shows the corridor connection between its two tenders. Judging by the body language of the crew, looking back along the train and with the loco letting off steam, it could be held at signals. The roster is the SLS/MLS's 'Durham Coast Rail Tour', Huddersfield to Tyne Dock and return.
Chris Davies/www.railphotoprints.co.uk

Below: **TYNE DOCK** During a break in the itinerary of the 7 September tour, No 63395 is seen inside Tyne Dock shed. New from Darlington Works in December 1918 as No NER 2238, it was renumbered 3395 in the LNER's mass sort-out of its loco stock in 1946, and was eventually another to find sanctuary in preservation.
Chris Davies/www.railphotoprints.co.uk

Bottom right: **HATTON** Another view of No 4472 *Flying Scotsman*, heading downhill at Hatton on Sunday 29 September 1968, with the British Railways Board's 'Tyseley Open Day Special', running to Leamington Spa and back. Meanwhile others enjoyed the delights of Tyseley Open Day. *Peter Fitton*

Left: **PLAWSWORTH VIADUCT**
'Peak' No D77 *Royal Irish Fusilier*, with its split headcode box, crosses Plawsworth Viaduct, County Durham, southbound with 3M27, an unidentified inter-regional working on 7 September 1968.
Chris Davies/www.railphotoprints.co.uk

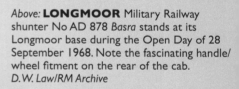

Above: **LONGMOOR** Military Railway shunter No AD 878 *Basra* stands at its Longmoor base during the Open Day of 28 September 1968. Note the fascinating handle/wheel fitment on the rear of the cab.
D. W. Law/RM Archive

Left: **SALISBURY** Its working life over, rebuilt 'Merchant Navy' 4-6-2 No 35030 *Elder Dempster Lines* sits in Salisbury Yard awaiting its final journey, to Buttigieg's scrapyard in Newport, in September 1968. New from Eastleigh Works on 16 April 1949, to the original 'air-smoothed' design, it was rebuilt to its final shape on 26 April 1958.
www.railphotoprints.co.uk collection

October

Above right: **TROWELL JUNCTION** Still in its original two-tone green livery, BR Class 47 No D1514 leaves the Erewash Valley line at Trowell Junction with a Sheffield-St Pancras express on 19 October 1968. The ex-MR signal box and first coach both look as though they have seen better days! The loco emerged from Brush Engineering's Falcon Works, Loughborough, in March 1963, going to 34G (Finsbury Park) depot. It was withdrawn in April 1987 and cut up in Vic Berry's Leicester scrapyard in June 1990. *V. Bamford/RM Archive*

Above Left: **AVIEMORE** With just a slight wisp of diesel exhaust hugging the carriage roofs, two BR Class 24s, sequentially numbered D5131 and D5132, head north from Aviemore through the wide open spaces towards Carrbridge with the 09.30 Glasgow Queen Street to Inverness express on 3 October 1968. *John M. Boyes/Armstrong Railway Photographic Trust*

Left: **LEICESTER MIDLAND SHED**. A sad day in October 1968 for Leicester steam enthusiasts, as the relatively young coaling tower (less than 20 years old) is being demolished by Contractors Hiring Company, with debris scattered across the adjacent tracks. Note the equally young steam roundhouse in the background. This would suffer the same fate in the not too distant future. *Peter Simmonds*

Right: **CROMDALE** Industrial steam has been an acquired taste for many, but the often more diminutive loco size and a need to work hard can give stunning results. A wonderful show of smoke and steam emits from SMD Co Barclay No 2020 (1936) as it climbs from Cromdale Goods Yard with wagons of empty casks for Balmenach Distillery on 1 October 1968.
John M. Boyes/Armstrong Railway Photographic Trust

Below: **KINGUSSIE** BR Class 27 No D5383 heads the 13.00 Perth Yard-Inverness freight through Kingussie station on 3 October 1968. The box vans make a lovely uniform length behind the loco as they pass through on the loop line. Has the driver of the Land Rover chosen parking under cover? *John M. Boyes/Armstrong Railway Photographic Trust*

Left: **KING'S CROSS** After the 'Fifteen Guinea Special' ran on 11 August 1968, BR banned all steam working across its standard-gauge network. A previous agreement between BR and Alan Pegler allowed ex-LNER 'A3' 'Pacific' No 4472 *Flying Scotsman* to run on BR for several more months. Here the engine, along with its two tenders, leaves King's Cross with the 'Yorkshire Harvester' to York via Knottingley on Sunday 6 October 1968. The special was run to raise funds for York Minster and returned to King's Cross up the East Coast Main Line. *Phil Horton*

Right: **GLOUCESTER** BR Class 22 No D6320 sits in the shed yard at Horton Road, Gloucester, on 19 October 1968. Fresh from the North British Locomotive Co in April 1960, this Type 2 was sent immediately to Laira (Plymouth) depot. The class was not very successful and this example was withdrawn in May 1971 and scrapped in Swindon Works in June 1972. *N. E. Preedy/RM Archive*

CRIGGLESTONE The viaduct at Calder Grove (known as Crigglestone Viaduct) boasts 21 arches and measures 1,270 feet in length. The most eastern arch sits over the Wakefield-Barnsley railway line, while the former Crigglestone Curve, (Crigglestone Junction to Horbury Station Junction), passed beneath its western approach embankment. The central section, seen here, towered over William Pepper & Son's British Oak site, with the old line serving the collieries around Flockton.

On 16 November 1968 a group of enthusiasts come to photograph the solitary 'Jinty' No 47445 seemingly abandoned among the sidings. New in 1927 from Hunslet, Leeds, it was a loyal loco in BR service, serving only Alsager (to 16 July 1960) and Crewe South sheds, the latter until withdrawal on 23 April 1966. 1970 saw it move for preservation at Butterley.

HAWORTH Earlier that same day the Leicester enthusiasts' group had visited the nascent Keighley & Worth Valley Railway at Haworth. In company with No 46115 *Scots Guardsman* and No 41241, far more ancient No 957 (ex-BR No 52044) awaits remedial attention, to become mobile like its two companions. Built by Beyer Peacock in 1887, Works No 2840, it initially served as L&YR No 957. A Goole shed resident between 1921 and 1948, it moved soon after nationalisation to Wakefield, where it stayed until withdrawal on 13 June 1959, having travelled 1,154,163 miles during its life. Preservation at the K&WVR was from March 1965. *Both MJS*

Right: **HAWORTH** Another valuable locomotive saved from the cutter's torch is prototype 'Crab' No 42700. New from Horwich Works on 19 June 1926, as No 13000, it was renumbered by the LMS to 2700 on 30 November 1934. Serving the Leeds area under BR until February 1956, it then became the property of the Manchester/Liverpool conurbations. Finally arriving at Birkenhead on 6 November 1965, the end came on 26 March 1966. Recognised as a strategic engine, it was acquired for preservation by the National Railway Museum. *MJS*

HEREFORD Another iconic loco, No 6000 *King George V*, had a colourful railway career after emerging new from Swindon Works on 29 June 1927, not least being shipped to the Baltimore & Ohio Railroad centenary exhibition in the September and being adorned with a large bell in front of the smokebox. Its active career ceased on 3 December 1962, after which it languished for a long period in Swindon Works scrapyard. Finally, salvation came from Bulmer's in Hereford, which took possession in November 1968, and its seen here on the 16th of that month, on the company's private line, giving rides in five Pullman cars. *N. E. Preedy/RM Archive*

Above: **HAWORTH** Another view of No 42700 in Haworth shed yard on 16 November 1968. Seemingly in steam and raring to go, the exhaust is actually from another loco across the yard.

Right: **HAWORTH** Another engine on shed is awaiting its turn for attention. The front number of 43924 is just visible in this view, half in and half out of the shed and with the chimney 'ragged' to help preserve its internal condition. Completed at Derby Works in October 1920, it initially worked from Wellingborough, but at nationalisation it was a resident of Gloucester (Barnwood). Its only other move was to Bristol (Barrow Road) on 8 September 1962, from where its end came on 11 July 1965. Transported to Barry Docks by September, it was an early escapee, moving to Haworth shortly before this picture was taken. *Both MJS*

Above: **PETTS WOOD** From iconic locos to an iconic train, the 'Golden Arrow' express. Known as the 'Flèche d'Or' in France, it was a luxury boat train of the Southern Railway and later British Railways. From 1929 it linked London with Dover, where passengers took the ferry to Calais to join the 'Flèche d'Or' through France. In 1951 a new set of Pullman cars was built for the service, exhibited as part of British Railways' celebration of the Festival of Britain. Ten years on, in 1961, with the Kent Coast electrification scheme, the train became electric-hauled, allowing an acceleration to the service. However, a decline in demand for rail travel between London and Paris saw the last 'Golden Arrow' run on 30 September 1972. By then, only the 1st Class section was advertised as a Pullman service. On 23 November 1968 DC electric No E5006 passes Petts Wood with the down 'Golden Arrow'. *www.railphotoprints.co.uk collection*

Above: **BRIGHTON** Another special train was the 'Brighton Belle'. On 21 December 1968 set No 3053 approaches its Brighton destination as it runs through Preston Park cutting. Notice how all tracks were weed-free in those days! *R. Collen-Jones/Rail Photoprints*

Left: **PETTS WOOD** Southern Region Class 73 No E6046 passes Petts Wood with what is believed to be the Dover Marine - Hither Green vans on 23 November 1968. *www.railphotoprints.co.uk collection*

SHANKEND BRC&W Type 2 No D5326 runs into Shankend station with a Carlisle-Edinburgh Waverley Route service in November 1968. Built in May 1959, the loco's first allocation was to Scotland, at Haymarket, unlike the first 20 of the class, which were initially employed from Hornsey depot. In November 1960 it moved north to Inverness, was renumbered 26026 in February 1974, and there it stayed until withdrawal on 24 November 1992. *Chris Davies/www.railphotoprints.co.uk*

Left: **ACTON YARD** On Wednesday 11 December 1968, a bleak, cold day, the UCL Railway Society had paid for two brake vans to be attached to a freight from Severn Tunnel Junction to Stratford at Acton Yard, West London. In this view, prior to the arrival of the freight, a variety of WR diesel-hydraulics and an ER diesel-electric can be seen in the gloom. On the left is a WR Type 2 (briefly Class 22) loco, while to its right are two WR Type 3 'Hymeks' (briefly Class 35). On the right is ER Type 2 No D5569 (later No 31151/31436). In the event the scheduled freight was stopped at Reading by a hot axle box on one of the wagons. However, with the agreement of its driver, No D5569, which was waiting to run light engine to Stratford, was attached to the brake vans and conveyed the party, along with a BR Inspector, around the North London Line rather more quickly than had been anticipated. *Phil Horton*

Below: **LUDGERSHALL** BR Class 33 No 6545 (later No 33027 from January 1974) passes through Ludgershall station with the daily return freight to Andover on 30 December 1968. Built by BRC&W in March 1961, it was graced with a naming, *Earl Mountbatten of Burma* (at Waterloo on 2 August 1980) until August 1989. Note the removal of a former platform on the right. *G. F. Gillham/RM Archive*

Above: **REDRUTH** The engines fire up as No D1041 *Western Prince* restarts its journey at Redruth with an up Penzance-Paddington service on Boxing Day 1968. Six years old at this stage, it would not last a whole lot longer, being withdrawn in February 1977, falling foul of BR(WR)'s antipathy to hydraulic traction – truly a waste of investment in these fine machines. *John Chalcraft/www.railphotoprints.co.uk*

Right: **PHILADELPHIA SHED** 1923-vintage, ex-LNER 'J27' No 5894 (erstwhile LNER No 2392 and BR No 65894) and Vulcan Foundry No 59 (No 5300/1945) undergo steaming tests at Philadelphia shed, NCB No 2 Area, on 13 December 1968. The sole survivor of a class of 115 locos, the 'J27' went on to see preservation with the NELPG at Darlington. Note the absence of boiler cladding during this test.
John M. Boyes/Armstrong Railway Photographic Trust

Below: **PHILADELPHIA SHED** While those two locos were being steam-tested for future use, the opposite is sadly in play here as NCB 0-6-2T No 10 is being cut up outside the shed at Philadelphia on 23 December 1968. For anyone who has not been privy to the cutting of locos, they would probably be aghast at the amount of debris, engine parts and detritus that surrounds such operations. It was ever thus, in BR Works, industrial sites or as here at Vic Berry's scrapyard in Leicester, but somehow the work was done with a minimum of injuries. *I. S. Carr/Armstrong Railway Photographic Trust*

ST ALBANS (?) To end our journey through 1968 we thought this image from that year provided an appropriate ending.

For so many railway enthusiasts old enough to remember, the end of standard-gauge steam on Britain's railways marked a significant milestone in their lives. Hundreds of railway photographers simply stopped taking pictures – not for them the un-alive and un-interesting diesel and electric boxes on wheels. They may have been the 'new age of the train', but they simply did not cut the mustard.

Gone were the living and breathing locomotives that provided dramatic and powerful images of hard-working machines billowing smoke as they climbed the gradients, gone were the pulsing motions of the pistons driving those varieties of wheel arrangements from the diminutive 0-4-0s through the 0-6-0s, the 0-6-2s, the 2-6-2s, the 4-6-0s and the 4-6-2s to the last of them all, *Evening Star*, representing the 2-10-0s .

No longer would we witness the delight of standing on a platform as a steam locomotive approached at speed and thundered past with its motion a blur as the driving wheels rotated at what seemed an impossible speed, only for it to disappear into the distance with the tail lamp of the last carriage flickering. As the saying goes, 'An elephant never forgets'. So too was 1968 for railway enthusiasts of a certain age!
Ray Ruffell/Slip Coach PS Archive

Index of locations